SECRET WINCHESTER

Anne-Louise Barton &
Elizabeth Hill-Goulding

AMBERLEY

First published 2018

Amberley Publishing
The Hill, Stroud
Gloucestershire, GL5 4EP

www.amberley-books.com

Copyright © Anne-Louise Barton &
Elizabeth Hill-Goulding, 2018

The right of Anne-Louise Barton &
Elizabeth Hill-Goulding to be identified as the
Authors of this work has been asserted in accordance
with the Copyrights, Designs and Patents Act 1988.

ISBN 978 1 4456 7185 7 (print)
ISBN 978 1 4456 7186 4 (ebook)

British Library Cataloguing in Publication Data.
A catalogue record for this book is available from the
British Library.

Origination by Amberley Publishing.
Printed in Great Britain.

Contents

Introduction

Winchester has a long and glorious past. With more than 2,000 years of history, the city's rich heritage is impressive and colourful. It was once England's capital with a royal palace, a bishop's palace and a Norman castle. It has witnessed royal weddings, births and baptisms. However, despite the regal pomp and ceremony, the city has also experienced devastation and decline caused by civil war and sieges, plagues and persecution. There was a brief moment in the seventeenth century when Winchester looked as if it would regain its glory days with Christopher Wren's commission from Charles II to build a palace to rival Versailles. How different things could have been if the king had not died before the palace was complete, and how different the cityscape would have looked with a grand boulevard stretching from Castle Hill to the cathedral.

Winchester today is a relatively quiet cathedral city nestled in the Itchen Valley, on the edge of the South Downs National Park. Many visitors are drawn to King Alfred's statue in the Broadway, the Great Hall, and Jane Austen's final resting place; these are well described in many other guidebooks. But what of the other, more hidden aspects of Winchester's history, and how do they link with what we already know?

In *Secret Winchester* we have selected histories, tales and themes that offer a new perspective. Starting with Winchester's ancient origins we explore the river and how it shaped the city. We focus on queens rather than kings, discover where the bodies lie, and how different religious faiths worked and lived together. We witness murders and executions. We go to the races and the theatre, and meet some Victorian entrepreneurs who helped to make the city what it is today.

Researching Winchester's history has brought to light a wealth of stories and information. These have given us a greater appreciation of the rich heritage that surrounds tourists and residents alike in this beautiful cathedral city.

1. The City and the River

Ancient Origins

Winchester High Street is one of the oldest streets in Britain. It follows the well-worn path of Iron Age Britons making their way down to a crossing point on the flood plain of a river. The river, now known as the Itchen, runs in a valley between chalk ridgeways that served as prehistoric routeways. Thirteen foreign coins dating from the third and second centuries BC have been found in and around Winchester, including ten from Egypt. These coins point to the fact that the ridgeways and the river crossing lay along ancient, long-distance communication routes. The geographical location of this crossing led to some form of early settlement and, eventually, the construction of enclosed hillforts on nearby raised ground.

Winchester High Street follows an ancient track from Oram's Arbour down to the river.

Students enjoying quidditch on Oram's Arbour, known to have been a significant Iron Age enclosure.

Burials and pieces of pottery dating from between 1,500 and 800/700 BC have been found on eight sites in Winchester and pottery from a later date, perhaps between 700 and 300 BC, has been discovered in the western part of the city. Outside the city, the remains of a hillfort have been found on St Catherine's Hill; the enclosure is thought to have been constructed during the Early to Middle Iron Age. It was destroyed by fire and abandoned before the Late Iron Age. From around the later Middle Iron Age, c. 150 BC, there existed an enclosure on the western bank of the Itchen. Now known as Oram's Arbour, this area of 20 ha (50 acres) was four times larger than the majority of hillforts from the Middle Iron Age. The High Street traces an ancient path from Oram's Arbour to the ford across the Itchen, located where the High Street now meets Colebrook Street. At this point ancient Britons were able to cross to a midstream island. The island is where, over 700 years later, King Cenwealh of Wessex built a church that was to become Old Minster, the outlines of which can be seen lying next to today's cathedral.

Venta Belgarum

By AD 70 the Romans were occupying the western bank of the Itchen near the Iron Age enclosure, together with the area now known as the Brooks, and the island which lay midstream. They named the settlement Venta Belgarum, 'the market place of the Belgae people', after the Belgae, the people whose land they had taken. Ambitious in their plans, the Romans set to work diverting the course of the river, effectively moving it eastwards. The Romans organised drainage channels in the area of the Brooks, they built bridges and extended the small islands lying within the river's flood plain. In addition to creating land upon which to build, they created ditch and rampart defences along the southern, western and northern sides of the town. Eventually, in the third century, the Romans built a 3-metre-wide stone wall in place of their earthwork defences. The line of this wall can be traced in property boundaries today; for example, in the garden walls between Canon Street and St Swithun Street. A small piece of Roman wall can still be seen on the eastern side of the city at The Weirs.

The Romans made full use of the flowing waters of the Itchen for both work and leisure. They built an aqueduct to supply piped water to some of their grander houses and, as Venta Belgarum was the fifth largest Roman town in Britain, it must be assumed that this water was also piped into public baths. The free-flowing energy of the river was harnessed to serve many mills. These drove industries such as weaving and the tanning of leather as well as grinding corn into flour. It is thought that Winchester's City Mill was originally established on the site of an earlier Roman mill.

The City Mill appears in Domesday as the mill of the Abbess of Wherwell. In 1554 it was given as a gift to the city by Mary Tudor.

The Anglo-Saxons

From the mid-fourth century the Roman town of Venta started to collapse. The drainage system eventually fell into disrepair, leaving the ground marshy and liable to flood. As a consequence the residents moved to the midstream island and the drier western slopes of the town. After the departure of the Romans in the fifth century most of the city's buildings became overgrown. When the Anglo-Saxons arrived they created settlements around the Winchester area; the new arrivals are likely to have used the river crossing. It has been suggested that within the old Roman walls there may have existed an area for the use of noble, royal or religious persons. It is also possible that the city retained its significance as a marketplace. Until more archaeological excavation can be undertaken, this is a time that still holds its secrets. Only a few pieces of Anglo-Saxon pottery dating from the fifth and sixth centuries have been found, so it is with King Cenwalh, 643–72, and the building of Old Minster that the known story of Winchester can be resumed.

Winchester became an important centre for Anglo-Saxon life, but it wasn't until the time of King Alfred in the late 800s that an engineering project, similar to that of the Romans, took place. Alfred organised the channelling of the meandering streams crossing the floodplain. These channels, which became known as the Lower, Middle and Upper Brooks, joined in St George's Street and then flowed across the High Street beside Cross Keys Passage. If standing on the right spot, the sound of the joined waters flowing beneath the lower part of the High Street can still be heard. This is true of several other places

The Coytebury flowing in front of Abbey Gardens. Its waters once powered a fulling mill.

where Winchester's old streams have been paved over; the planning brief for development in this part of the city is to open up some of these culverted streams. The Lockburn is a Saxon stream, now covered, which still follows a course through the Cathedral Close. It is thought this stream was diverted by St Aethelwold, Bishop of Winchester from 963 to 984, to provide a constant source of clean, running water to the monastic buildings within the Cathedral Close. Wolfstan, a contemporary monk, wrote of Aethelwold that he 'brought here sweet streams of fishful water, and an overflow of the stream passed through the inner part of the monastic buildings, cleansing the whole monastery with its murmur'. (*The Waterways of Winchester*, City of Winchester Trust, Spring 1994)

Aethelwold diverted the stream to run through the monks' lavatorium, in an area that is now the Dean's garden. This conduit served the monks' 'necessarium' or communal latrine, where excavations have discovered that they could seat forty-six monks at any one time!

A Medieval Dispute

By medieval times the water channels of Winchester had become polluted with the detritus of the day, including dyes from the wool and leather industries, animal blood and entrails, and human waste. Around 1300, a dispute in Winchester over access to clean water brought about a legal decision which, having been passed down the centuries, is now enshrined in the United Nations Convention of Human Rights. The case involved two neighbours: the wealthy John de Tytyng and a laundress, Juliana de la Floude. John de

Middle Brook Street, painted by Samuel Prout in 1813.

Tytyng was twice mayor of Winchester and twice its MP. He owned a comparatively luxurious property in Shulworth Street, now known as Upper Brook Street. John de Tytyng objected to Juliana running her medieval launderette in the public stream running along Shulworth Street and tried to block off her water supply. With her source of livelihood in danger, Juliana appealed to King Edward I, who appointed a commission to look into the matter. Following the commission's report King Edward declared that 'water has always been common', meaning that water always had been, and always should be, accessible to all people. The commission also recommended that the water should not be contaminated by the dyes and other forms of waste that had become such a problem for the health of Winchester's medieval residents.

A Working River

The River Itchen, together with its tributary streams, was essential to the economic life of Winchester. Records show that in 1208 there were twenty-two mills between Hyde Abbey and St Cross. The waters provided energy for these mills and also a means of transporting goods the 20 kilometres (12.5 miles) between Winchester and Southampton, and thence on to the Continent. This was particularly useful for moving heavy goods, such as building materials, and it is possible that the Caen stone used in the building of the cathedral was transported along the river. The name Wharf Hill is a reminder of the days when goods could be brought into the city in this way. The name Chesil Street, which connects to Wharf Hill, refers to the shingle beach that lay along the banks of the Itchen at this point. The word 'chesil' means pebble, as in the famous Chesil Beach in Dorset. In the late twelfth century the Bishop of Winchester, Godfrey de Lucy, funded improvements to the waterway and as a consequence was entitled to levy tolls on the transportation of goods, including the wool and leather that was largely responsible for Winchester's wealth. From the mid-fourteenth century Winchester's part in this trade declined and the navigable parts of the river fell into disrepair. Following an Act of Parliament passed in 1665, work commenced to improve the river for transportation. This involved bypassing difficult sections of the river by cutting stretches of canal and creating locks. By 1795 there were fifteen locks between Winchester and Southampton Water. The opening of the London–Southampton railway in 1840 meant that the Itchen Navigation was no longer financially viable and it once again fell into disrepair.

In recent years the Hampshire and Isle of Wight Wildlife Trust has worked with authorities such as the Environment Agency, Hampshire County Council and Winchester City Council to improve the Itchen Navigation, for the benefit of both wildlife and walkers. A footpath, the Itchen Way, has been created alongside the Navigation allowing walkers the chance to spot a variety of wildlife. The Itchen has crystal-clear waters due to its chalk bed and this rare environment provides a habitat for a variety of animals including trout, salmon, kingfishers and water voles. In addition, the river now provides a home for otters, since three were reintroduced back in 1994. Winchester's City Mill has observation equipment set up to capture the activity of the otters living along its stretch of water. Visitors to the mill can enjoy watching clips of footage and, with luck, have the chance to see an otter on the live feed from one of its cameras.

The Itchen Navigation viewed from Black Bridge at the bottom of Wharf Hill.

An inspirational setting. During his stay in Winchester in 1819 the poet John Keats took daily walks along the river and composed his ode 'To Autumn'.

DID YOU KNOW ?

The River Itchen flooded in 1852, 1903, 1928, 1935, 1947, 2001 and 2014. Following the Winchester floods of 2014, the City Council, County Council, Environment Agency and the University of Southampton worked together to build a £1m flood defence in order to protect the areas around River Park Leisure Centre, St Bede Church of England Primary School and the Winchester School of Art. The scheme includes reinforced brick walls and flood gates that can be operational within twenty minutes.

A footpath alongside the weirs closed during the 2014 Winchester floods.

2. Queenly Connections

Winchester's Anglo-Saxon Queens

Winchester was a favoured city of the Anglo-Saxon queens. It offered a safe haven in times of Viking attack, and was important as an economic and religious centre. The city was subject to a successful Viking raid in 860, but following King Alfred's defeat of the Danish army at the Battle of Edington in 878, and his fortification of many Wessex towns including Winchester, trade and industry thrived and the city became Alfred's capital. These factors made Winchester an attractive place to own property. Alfred granted his wife Ealhswith an estate in the south-eastern corner of Winchester, encompassing the area now known as Abbey Gardens and the Abbey Mill. Around the year 900, Ealhswith used the land for the building of a nuns' minster, or Nunnaminster, later known as St Mary's Abbey. The queen is likely to have established this religious community as both a personal legacy and a place in which she could retire from court and spend her final years, a tradition of widowed Anglo-Saxon queens. Ealhswith, who died in 902, would have had very little time to appreciate her new nuns' minster, but her granddaughter, Eadburga, was to become its most famous resident.

Abbey Gardens, site of Queen Ealhswith's Nunnaminster.

Tombs from Nunnaminster, situated in Abbey Passage, adjacent to the Guildhall.

As a young princess, Eadburga was said to have demonstrated her vocation by choosing a Bible and small chalice in preference to the jewellery that was offered to her, thus embracing a religious life over a royal marriage. At a very tender age she was placed in the care of the Abbess at Nunnaminster and was to live there for the remainder of her life. Eadburga was revered for her deeply held religious beliefs and the way in which she led a life of humility, exemplified by accounts of her washing the socks of her fellow nuns each evening! The reverence in which she was held continued following her death at the age of thirty; miracles were said to occur near her simple tomb and her fame spread. Eadburga quickly became recognised as a saint and eventually her remains were transferred to a far grander tomb decorated with precious metals and topaz. The cult of St Eadburga brought both prestige and income to Nunnaminster.

In 1012, King Aetheldred II gave a large estate within the city of Winchester to his young wife, Emma of Normandy. This gift delivered revenue directly to the queen. The manor was positioned on the north side of the High Street, at the western 'top end' of Winchester, and was in effect a trading centre that could organise its own laws, rents and taxes, free of interference from the mayor of Winchester or even the king. This manor was known as the 'Manor of Goudbeyete', or 'Godbiete', which has been interpreted as 'a house granted to God,' or 'a good bargain' or even 'the goods getter'. Upon her death in 1052, Queen Emma bequeathed the Got Begot manor to St Swithun's Priory. Within her bequest Emma stipulated that the manor was to be 'toll free and tax free for ever' and that no authority was to be recognised within the manor other than that of the Prior and Convent of St Swithun. This rendered the Got Begot manor a sanctuary for a variety of people including rogues and

Above left: The mock-Tudor frontage of the Godbegot was an addition of the early 1900s.

Above right: Emma and Cnut presenting a large gold cross to New Minster.

criminals right up until the reformation under Henry VIII. The current Godbegot House dates originally from 1462 but was rebuilt in 1558; substantial alterations and additions were made in the nineteenth and twentieth centuries. The site of Emma's chapel, St Peter's, can be seen outlined in brick on the pavement to the rear of the building.

The years of Emma's marriage to King Aethelred were dogged by Viking attacks, which ended in 1016 with a Danish victory. Cnut was crowned in Winchester's New Minster and, in an astute political move, the new king arranged to marry Aethelred's widow. The couple were married in Winchester and the city became Cnut and Emma's capital. They presented a gift of a huge gold cross to New Minster and, eventually, the couple were buried in Winchester's Old Minster. At a later date their bones were laid to rest in one of the cathedral's mortuary chests.

The last Anglo-Saxon queen to live in Winchester was Edward the Confessor's widow and Harold Godwinson's sister, the Dowager Queen Edith. Following the death of her mother-in-law, Queen Emma, Edith was given the title of 'the Lady' and was the richest woman in England. Lady Edith lived in Winchester and owned several manors and a considerable amount of property. Following the Norman invasion of 1066, she surrendered Winchester to William the Conqueror and as a consequence was allowed to live in peace in her house on the High Street until her death in 1075.

The Empress, the King, the Queen and the Bishop

The embittered struggle for the throne, which raged from 1135 until 1153, left England in a state of turmoil and destroyed much of medieval Winchester. The frequent battles and constant movement of troops left much of the English countryside desolate and resulted in famine. The origin of the saga lay with the tragic death of King Henry I's only legitimate son, William, who drowned at sea aged seventeen. In 1120, Prince William had just married and was returning to England from Normandy with his new bride when his ship struck rocks and sank. It is thought that the crew were drunk due to the wedding celebrations. The distraught king named his daughter Matilda, wife of Emperor Henry V of Germany, as his heir and asked the barons to swear oaths that on his death she would become Queen of England. These oaths were to be tested in the winter of 1135–36 when, on hearing of Henry I's death, his nephew, Stephen, seized the crown. The Empress Matilda was situated in Normandy and perhaps news of her father's death did not reach her as quickly as it reached the ears of her cousin in Boulogne. It has been suggested she may have been hampered by pregnancy, or perhaps, considering her English crown secure, the Empress Matilda did not sense the need to rush to England; this hesitation proved to be a fatal error.

The Westgate, scene of Matilda's triumphant entrance into Winchester.

Stephen seized the moment. With the aid of his brother, Bishop of Winchester Henry de Blois, Stephen quickly secured both the royal treasury and the throne. While the majority of barons broke their oath to King Henry and supported Stephen's cause, the Empress Matilda had sufficient followers to fight back. Years of unrest were to follow, with Henry de Blois at the heart of political manoeuvring. A pivotal moment in the struggle for power came in 1141 when King Stephen was captured at the Battle of Lincoln. With his brother held captive in Bristol, Bishop Henry switched sides and pledged his oath of allegiance to Matilda. It was Henry who was instrumental in Matilda's triumphant welcome into Winchester. Huge numbers of citizens watched her retinue as it passed through the West Gate and processed down the High Street and into the cathedral precinct. There she was met by the Bishops of St David's, Ely and Lincoln, and a few days later by Theobold, Archbishop of Canterbury, who had travelled to Winchester to meet with the empress and support her claim to the throne. With the swell of support behind her, Matilda progressed to London to prepare for her coronation at Westminster. However, her arrogant behaviour, which was seen as 'unbecoming' for a woman, coupled with her demands for taxes, quickly alienated her from the citizens of London.

With Stephen held captive, it was his queen, also called Mathilde, who now came into play. Queen Mathilde gathered troops and marched on London. The resulting violence caused the citizens to turn on the Empress Matilda, forcing her to flee before she could be crowned. At this point, Bishop Henry deserted her and returned to Winchester where

Wolvesey Palace was damaged but not destroyed during the siege of Winchester. It continued to be maintained as a bishop's residence until the 1640s.

he quickly set about fortifying his palace at Wolvesey. After learning of his betrayal, the empress led her army to Winchester. On 31 July 1141 she seized control of Winchester Castle and from there she besieged Wolvesey Palace, perhaps not knowing that the Bishop had already slipped away. Henry sent word to Queen Mathilde whose troops soon advanced on Winchester and encircled the city. The besiegers were now besieged. In those first few days of August 1141, almost half the city was destroyed by fire. Around twenty-three churches were damaged or destroyed. The old royal palace, which lay in the line of fire between the castle and Wolvesey, was decimated. The queen's army looted homes and shops and took captives. For more than a month they prevented supplies from reaching the castle where the Empress Matilda was positioned. The attack on Winchester lasted until 14 September when the empress fled the city, which now lay in ruins. With the queen's supporters in pursuit, Matilda rode hard to Devizes with her half-brother, Robert of Gloucester, fighting a rearguard action. Robert was captured and subsequently exchanged for King Stephen. It seemed that the struggle for the throne was endless, with neither side having the strength to deal the fatal blow to the other. However, Matilda's cause was aided by the deaths of Queen Mathilde in 1152 and King Stephen's son Eustace in 1153. It was at this point that Bishop Henry de Blois successfully mediated between King Stephen, Empress Matilda and her son Prince Henry. This resulted in the Treaty of Winchester, in which King Stephen agreed that Prince Henry would become his heir. It was with the Treaty of Winchester that peace could at last be restored to England.

The Treaty of Winchester passed the crown from King Stephen (on the left) to Prince Henry (right), the Empress Matilda's son.

A Royal Wedding

A glittering highlight in the story of Winchester is the wedding in 1554 of Mary Tudor, aged thirty-eight, to the twenty-seven-year-old Philip of Spain, son of the Emperor Charles V. This wedding was intended to unite the two countries and herald a new dawn for the 'old faith' which Mary's father and brother had done so much to destroy. One reason that Winchester was chosen as the venue for the ceremony was the belief that its residents were more willing to accept a return to Catholism than the population of London; indeed its bishop, Stephen Gardiner, was an ardent supporter of Mary's plans.

Philip disembarked at Southampton on Friday 20 July 1554. He is reported to have 'made merry' for a few days and nights with his Spanish entourage and a gathering number of illustrious English gentlemen. He left for Winchester on the following Monday in the pouring rain, accompanied by 3,000–4,000 Spanish and English nobles and cavalry guards. Accounts of the prince's arrival in Winchester differ: some say he rode straight to the cathedral while others report that upon reaching the outskirts of Winchester, the prince dismounted at St Cross Hospital and went in to change out of his travelling clothes. On reaching the city gates the prince was met by officials dressed in scarlet who ceremonially gave him the keys of the city and its castle. After a tour of the cathedral the prince was taken to his lodgings at the Deanery. That night he was taken privately to Wolvesey Palace for his first meeting with Mary, his wife to be. Juan De Varaona, thought to be one of the Spanish party, describes Wolvesey as having 'a flower garden and orchard' and a 'winding stairway' leading to the hall where the queen waited for her betrothed (p.97 Himsworth). Andres Munoz, a contemporary, although not one of the Spanish visitors, recounts a description of the prince and his accompanying gentlemen walking across the lawns of Wolvesey gardens and seeing 'fountains, marvellous flowing streams, and diversity of scented flowers and trees and other delights of verdure' (p.85 Himsworth). Wolvesey Palace itself is described by Pedro Enriquez, part of the Spanish retinue, as being 'well dressed with heavy brocades and rich tapestries of gold' (p.92 Himsworth).

Mary I, painted by Hans Eworth c. 1556.

The wedding took place from 11 a.m. until 3 p.m. on 25 July, the feast day of St James, patron saint of Spain. The interior of the cathedral was adorned with 'many sumptuous cloths of brocade and crimson and of dark colours', and was 'full of banners and standards' (*p.98 Himsworth*). The brackets upon which these rich tapestries were hung are still in place today. Within the cathedral a raised path led to a dais, covered in red and gold silk, upon which the marriage ceremony took place; this allowed the packed congregation a clear view of the royal couple. The citizens of Winchester and the surrounding area flocked to witness the spectacle. Here was a chance to see not only the queen, but nobles and knights from many countries, including Germany, Hungary, Bohemia, Poland and India. There were at least fifty ladies from the nobility dressed in clothes of gold and silver, richly adorned with precious stones. The queen herself wore a skirt woven with gold thread, a black velvet gown bordered with gold braid, a train of gold cloth and a black velvet headdress covered with pearls. Some sources mention a purple embroidered gown but this may have been the dress she wore the day before the wedding. Mary wore a flat diamond with a large pearl pendant – a wedding gift from Philip. The Spanish prince wore a white coat bordered with silver braid and an outer robe woven with gold thread, embellished with precious stones and pearls. He wore a black velvet cap decked with

The chair said to have been used by Mary during the long wedding ceremony.

white feathers. During the lengthy ceremony Mary was able to rest on a chair, which had been sent as a gift from Rome. The folding chair was covered in blue or purple velvet from Genoa and had silver mounted finials. It is now an important possession of today's cathedral. Following the ceremony, the expectant crowds waiting outside were treated to the sight of the newly married couple walking to Wolvesey Palace beneath a canopy borne by seven knights. A grand wedding banquet was held at the Bishop's palace, followed by a ball where the Spanish and English nobility, together with ambassadors from many other countries, mingled.

Following the celebrations, where did all the wedding guests sleep? Many will have been accommodated in official residences but even so, Winchester's inns, estimated to be around one hundred in number, were filled to capacity by visitors for the royal wedding. Enriquez reports that the Spanish visitors faced difficulties in finding accommodation, stating 'only the early comer gets good lodgings' (p.93 Himsworth). Enriquez also reports that some were robbed on the way to Winchester by the 'great rogues' who 'infest these roads' (p.93 Himsworth). Crime was not limited to the open highway; four or five boxes are reported to have gone missing from the Prince's lodgings. After spending six nights at Wolvesey Palace the royal couple left Winchester. Their retinue was not able to depart en masse as there were not enough lodgings along the route to accommodate such a multitude.

At the time of Mary Tudor's wedding, Winchester was no longer a wealthy city and so it was necessary for money to be sent from London to aid with the costs. Listed in those costs are 5 shillings for painting the Lord Chancellor's coat of arms on the West Gate and 19 shillings for restoration work on the Buttercross, an important Winchester icon even in the Tudor era. Following the wedding, Mary showed her gratitude to the city by granting rents from former monastic properties to the city corporation, thereby doubling its income. The outcome of the wedding was not to be so felicitous for Mary. The queen's hopes of a fruitful marriage securing a Catholic dynasty were to turn to dust when her pregnancy turned out to be false and Philip returned to Spain. She was to die four years after her wedding.

DID YOU KNOW ?

Winchester has connections with three Queen Eleanors: Queen Eleanor of Aquitaine (c. 1122–04), mother of Richard the Lionheart and the infamous King John, was kept under house arrest in Winchester and Sarum by her husband Henry II; Eleanor of Provence (1223–91) was married to Henry III who oversaw the building of the Great Hall. Henry spent money on improving the royal apartments within the castle and built a herb garden in its grounds for his queen. Eleanor of Provence's daughter-in-law, Eleanor of Castile (c. 1246–90), also spent time living at Winchester's castle. In 1986, HM the Queen Mother opened 'Queen Eleanor's garden', a re-creation of a medieval castle garden, situated on the south side of the Great Hall.

The bronze falcon in Queen Eleanor's Garden, adjacent to the Great Hall.

3. Pastimes and Leisure

The Sport of Kings

There is a tale of Athelstan, grandson of Alfred the Great, being presented with a number of German-bred racehorses in Winchester as a gift in connection with the marriage of one of his sisters. A favourite national pastime, horse racing undoubtedly started in Winchester a long time ago, and continued down the centuries with differing measures of popularity. Racing calendars did not start until 1727, but there is evidence of meetings before this date as in his *History of Newmarket and Annals of the Turf* (1886), the author J. P. Hoare talks of Lord Pembroke making 'extraordinary great winnings at a horse-race in Winchester' in 1631. After the Civil War and upon the Restoration, the Winchester Races flourished with the support of Charles II who, after visiting the city in 1682 and attending the races, made plans for a new 'King's House' to be built. He instructed Sir Christopher Wren to work on the palace, but sadly the king died three years later and the building was left unfinished. Winchester, however, retained its enthusiasm for this pastime.

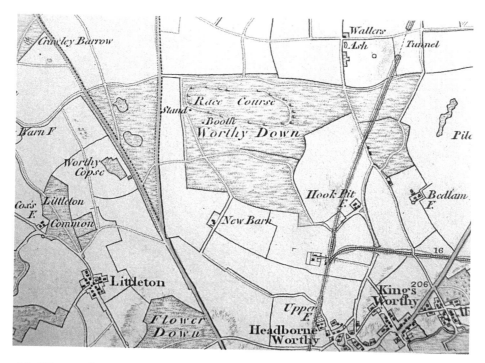

1867 OS map of Hampshire showing the location of the Winchester racecourse on Worthy Down, with its stand and booth.

Horse racing formed part of the entertainment for another royal occasion when Queen Anne and her consort visited in 1705. The extensive course was 2 miles in length with a 6 furlong straight, much of it uphill. It was located 4 miles north of Winchester, near the village of South Wonston and close to where the Worthy Down army camp is now situated. The road that once led from the Westgate to the racecourse, now Sussex Street, was known as Race Way.

The racing season brought a flurry of activity and a boost in trade for the city. The runners were entered several days before the race event, and this often took place at one of two inns on the High Street: The Chequer's Inn, which occupied a large site opposite the Buttercross (up until 1769 when it was demolished), and The White Hart Inn, next to the old Guildhall building. Cockfighting would have taken place at many of the inns in Winchester, and 'ordinaries' served. This was a fixed-price meal served up at around 2 p.m. so everyone was nicely sated before the races, which usually commenced between 4 and 5 p.m. There was something for everyone in and around the city, as other social events included concerts and balls for the genteel and aristocratic, who came in their finery to spend money.

On 15 July 1817, from her room in College Street, an ailing Jane Austen was to write her last poem, which she entitled 'Venta'. Coinciding with St Swithun's Day, she playfully admonishes the lively crowds who flocked to Worthy Down, and imagines the saint cursing them, promising that from then on, their race meetings will be accompanied by rain.

Venta
When Winchester races first took their beginning
It is said the good people forgot their old Saint
Not applying at all for the leave of St Swithin
And that William of Wykeham's approval was faint.

The races however were fix'd and determin'd
The company met & the Weather was charming
The Lords & the Ladies were sattin'd & ermin'd
And nobody saw any future alarming.

But when the old Saint was inform'd of these doings
He made but one Spring from his Shrine to the roof
Of the Palace which now lies so sadly in ruins
And thus he address'd them all standing aloof.

'Oh, subjects rebellious! Oh Venta depraved
When once we are buried you think we are dead
But behold me Immortal. - By vice you're enslaved
You have sinn'd and must suffer. - Then further he said

These races & revels & dissolute measures
With which you're debasing a neighboring Plain
Let them stand – you shall meet with your curse in your pleasures
Set off for your course, I'll pursue with my rain.

Ye cannot but know my command in July.
Henceforward I'll triumph in shewing my powers,
Shift your race as you will it shall never be dry
The curse upon Venta is July in showers.

The last account of the races in Winchester was reported in the *Hampshire Chronicle* in July 1887, although the grandstand existed until 1917. Reasons for the decline of horse racing might be attributed to the coming of the railways, with more accessible courses being favoured, or the Jockey Club rule that every race after 1877 must be worth a clear £100 to the winner. There is now nothing to indicate where so many years of this 'Sport of Kings' took place. But nearby, at Farley Mount, there is a memorial to a famous horse owned by Paulet St John Esq, which in 1733 fell into a chalk pit 25 feet deep whilst on a fox hunt. They both survived and went on to win the Hunter's Cup at the races in October the following year. The horse was entered under his new name of 'Beware Chalk-Pit'.

1860s illustration of the horse monument on Farley Mount, at a time when the races were still running a few miles away.

DID YOU KNOW ?

The first record of a pub on the site of the former White Hart Inn was in the fifteenth century. The current building dates back to 1806 when innkeeper John Bell commissioned local architect George Moneypenny to rebuild it. The balcony was a favourite spot for visiting politicians to address their public; in 1852 the Duke of Wellington spoke to the citizens of Winchester from here.

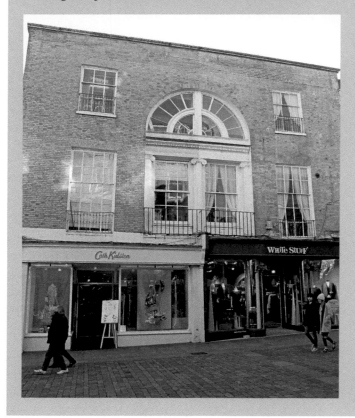

The former White Hart inn, which catered for pre-race gatherings.

Curtain-up

Winchester's first permanent theatre began entertaining its citizens on the upper floor of the Meat Market Hall situated in Market Square (on the site of the City Museum). On the ground floor there were around nine butchers' stalls and quarters for keeping pigs, cows and sheep. Stairs led to a room on the upper floor, which, by 1690, actors were hiring and charging admission to the public. This would have been a terribly noisy and smelly venue, with the public stocks outside in The Square only adding to the distractions. Rudimentary in those early years, with a rough platform and benches, improvements were made over the decades and in 1774 the *Hampshire Chronicle* reported that the proprietors of the theatre had 'spared no trouble or expense to render the Theatre warm and commodious'.

The City Museum stands on the site of the Meat Market Hall, home of Winchester's first permanent theatre.

In July 1784, costumes and sets of the Market House Theatre were packed for the last time due to a new venue being built on Jewry Street at a cost of £1,000, paid for by subscriptions raised amongst wealthy residents of the city. The architects were Kernot & Dowling, a local firm of coal merchants and builders, and the decorator was William Cave, a local artist whose talents were diverse. He was responsible for the restoration of the painted glass in Winchester College Chapel, some lettering in St Swithun's-Upon-Kingsgate, as well as painting landscapes, murals and a number of scene cloths for the theatre. New Theatre, as it became known, opened in 1785 with a production of Sheridan's *The Rivals*. Ten years earlier this comedy had received its first production at Covent Garden. The New Theatre's manager had chosen it as the opening play for his theatre in Salisbury in 1777, and so it was to be the opening play in Winchester also. Audiences paid three shillings for box seats, two shillings for pit seats and one shilling for the gallery. Interestingly, in 1797, a lack of punctuality was causing problems for the manager as although the starting time was advertised, the audience was frequently late. He was in a dilemma. It appeared the fullness of the theatre depended on the hour at which the last horse race was run, and so rather than playing to a sparse house, the actors decided to wait until people had travelled back from the races at Worthy Down.

New Theatre changed its name to the Theatre Royal in 1840 and its last performance was enjoyed in May 1861. The site on which the theatre stood was redeveloped in the 1980s, and the building seen today is called Sheridan House. A small section of the original theatre remained intact until the redevelopment started; unfortunately the façade collapsed onto the street. The red-bricked part of the new building was carefully reconstructed to the original design, with the added feature of a phoenix above the window.

Sheridan House on Jewry Street, where the New Theatre once stood. It opened in 1785 with a production of *The Rivals*.

Elegant Assembly Rooms

The tall, grand Georgian building of St John's House has played an important role and witnessed many gatherings, civic and social, over the centuries. It originally dates from the time of Edward I in the late thirteenth century, when the king licensed John Devenish, a citizen and alderman, to found the Hospital of St John's 'for the relief of sick and lame soldiers, poor pilgrims and necessitous wayfaring men'. The medieval building consisted of a refectory and kitchen on the ground floor, and a large hall which was used for municipal purposes on the first floor; the first record of such use was in 1284 when it was declared that every year upon the Monday following midsummer's day, the mayor and his brethren and all the corporation should meet at this house for supper.

Between 1768 and 1770, St John's House was completely reconstructed. The walls were raised by 6 feet, the lead roof replaced by a tiled one and the front remodelled with the addition of a parapet wall. The interior was completely refurbished to provide an Assembly Room described as 'the completest and most elegant public room in this part of the Kingdom, it contains five superb chandeliers and is richly ornamented with a variety of pleasing devices in stucco work. At the upper end there is a picture of King Charles II painted by the celebrated Sir Peter Lely'. (Wavell, *The History and Antiquities of Winchester*, 1773). Much of this original stucco plasterwork still remains and is a fine example of Regency craftsmanship. It would certainly have been admired by the wealthy citizens of the day who attended balls, dinners and concerts. Between 1788 and 1845 prominent musicians played here, including Niccolo Paganini and Franz Liszt.

When the new Guildhall was built in 1871, a grand banqueting hall was also included, and all municipal functions of the city were transferred across to the new Broadway venue.

St John's House has been the venue for many municipal functions and social gatherings over the centuries.

In 1845, the Archaeological Institute of Great Britain and Ireland held its annual meeting in St John's Rooms.

MEETING OF THE BRITISH ARCHÆOLOGICAL INSTITUTE, ST. JOHN'S WINCHESTER.

Pictures were stripped from the walls of St John's and rehung over the road; the introduction of gas lighting replaced the five chandeliers, and the room's glory was diminished.

During the twentieth century St John's House saw a variety of uses, including a concert hall, theatre, boxing booth and in the First World War, a forces' canteen. Between 1910 and 1914 John and James Simpkins leased the hall from the trustees of the charity with the idea of using it as a cine-variety theatre. It became the Palace Picture House and its opening season included the Belmoir Sisters with Coleman's Picture and Vaudeville Company, and amongst the first films screened were *At the Mercy of the Tide*, *Soap in Her Eyes* and *Betty's Removal*.

Thomas Stopher was surveyor to the trustees and in his notes of 1924 reported that the Corporation have 'placed on the First Floor a very beautiful and expensive Collection of British Birds, presented to the City by T.A.Cotton, Esq.'. The room was open to the public four days a week, and was also let for the purposes of lectures and public addresses. The old refectory on the ground floor was used as a waiting room by the Hants and Dorset Bus Company until 1935, when their new station was opened. Bob and Fred Chisnell, of the King Alfred Motor Company, took over the tenancy at St John's and established a parcel, enquiry and lost property office. They also sublet part of the ground floor to a Miss Smith, who ran a tearoom there.

Get Your Skates On

The King Alfred Motor Services had been started by the Chisnells' father, Robert Senior, who was quite the entrepreneur. In 1910 and early 1911, he hired the Corn Exchange on Jewry Street (now the Discovery Centre) and ran it as a roller-skating rink. His wife's brother-in-law, Mr Cobb, owned a farm near Winnall Moors, then a marshy area on the north side of the city. One winter it completely iced up, and so not wanting to miss the opportunity, the enterprising team of Mr Chisnell, Mr Cobb and a Mr Tebbett fenced off certain areas and charged the public a small sum to skate there. Winnall Moors is now a nature reserve managed by the Hampshire & Isle of Wight Wildlife Trust. It is a delightful pocket of countryside in the heart of the city.

Left and opposite above: Winter scenes at Winnall Moors Nature Reserve today.

DID YOU KNOW ?

In 1900, there were 132 pubs in Winchester, twenty-one of them on the High Street. There were also five breweries at that time.

Beaumond Green as it is today.

DID YOU KNOW ?

In Elizabethan times there was a large open space behind the cottages and gardens on Gold Street (Southgate Street) called Bewmonds, now Beaumond Green. It stretched up to the castle and here archery was practised. It later became a bowling green. The path up to the Green is called Archery Lane.

Taking us back to Elizabethan times.

4. Links with a Legend

King Arthur's Round Table, a vast wooden disk hanging on the wall of the Great Hall, has become an icon of the city of Winchester. The table, which is 5.5 metres (18 feet) in diameter and weighs 1,200 kg (1 ton 4 cwt), was first recorded as being in the Great Hall in the 1450s. Until research was undertaken in the 1970s by Professor Martin Biddle and his team, no one knew its true age, or if it had ever been used as a table at all.

In 1976, upon being removed from the wall and examined, it was discovered that the table top was made from fifty-one planks of wood from seven or eight oak trees. These planks were secured in the same way that a mill wheel was constructed. It was found that the table originally had twelve legs around the perimeter and a strong, central supporting leg, so it had indeed at one time served as an actual table. It is thought that these legs were removed in 1348 prior to the table being hung on display.

The historical detective work that took place in the 1970s revealed that the table wasn't quite as ancient as some people may have thought. A combination of radio-carbon dating and dendrochronology (the analysis of tree rings) dated the table from the late

Above left: Winchester's Round Table dates from the thirteenth century.

Above right: The table is made from 121 separate pieces of oak, with fifty-one thin planks forming the tabletop.

thirteenth century. Historians now believe that the table was made for Edward I, but there are differing opinions on the year the table was built and for what purpose. In September 1285 Edward I held a significant knighting ceremony in Winchester and the table may have been commissioned for this event, linking Edward's knights with the 'Knights of the Round Table' from Arthurian legend. Alternatively, the table may have been commissioned for the occasion of a royal tournament held in 1290 to celebrate the marriage of Edward's son to Margaret of Scotland and the proposed marriage of two of his daughters. During the tournament Winchester Castle received the Royal Court and the king's guests; it is quite possible that the table was built for the accompanying celebratory feasts. In both cases the purpose was the same: to bring about an association between the reign of Edward I and the legend of King Arthur. In France in the early thirteenth century, a trilogy of stories about Arthur known as the *Vulgate Cycle* appeared. The final story, *The Mort Artu*, describes a great tournament held on meadowland at Winchester. Lancelot and his companions ride 'until they come to the meadow of Winchester which was already completely covered with jousters' (Biddle & Badham, *King Arthur's Round Table*). Sixty years on from the writing of this story, Edward I and his wife, Queen Eleanor, both readers of Arthurian romance, held their royal tournament at Winchester. The exact location of the 1290 tournament is not known, but it may well have taken place in Hyde Meadows, just beyond the north wall.

The upstairs interior of WHSmith reminds visitors of Winchester's Camelot connection.

Hyde Meadows was a large area of land to the north of the city, encompassing the site of River Park Leisure Centre.

DID YOU KNOW ?

Edward III was evoking the chivalry of the Knights of the Round Table when he established the Order of the Garter in 1348. Edward based the new order of knighthood in Windsor, his place of birth, but made the Bishop of Winchester its religious leader in order to maintain its connection with Arthurian legend. The Bishop of Winchester continues to hold the office of Prelate of the Garter to this day.

The Camelot Connection

With King Arthur's Round Table in the Great Hall, at times referred to as Arthur's Hall, it is worth considering who *was* Arthur and did he have any links with the city of Winchester. Arthur has become a mythical figure but traces of actual events and real people may be bound up with the myth. Arthur may have been a single Celtic chieftain, but it seems more likely that the Arthurian legend embraces the combined stories of real figures dating back to the fifth and sixth centuries, perhaps earlier. His story symbolizes British resistance to the Saxons in the fifth century and the legend has been made greater in the retelling. On certain occasions British monarchs have found it useful to shore up power by tracing their ancestry back to this symbol of ancient and noble kingship. Much of the story of King Arthur occurs in locations to the west of Winchester: Glastonbury, Cornwall and Wales are obvious examples. However, Winchester does make an appearance every now and again. In his *Historia Regum Britanniae* (1135), Geoffrey of Monmouth writes that Uther Pendragon was at Winchester when he 'received the diadem of the Kingdom of Britain and was made King' (Biddle & Badham, *King Arthur's Round Table*). In 1155, Wace, a Norman, added to the legend by describing Arthur's battle against Mordred as happening somewhere outside Winchester. Arthur is said to have captured Winchester as Mordred fled to Southampton and thence on to Cornwall. Wace in his poem *Le Roman de Brut* introduced the idea of a round table into the Arthurian legend.

In 1460, Thomas Malory in his *Le Morte d'Arthur* suggested that Winchester was Camelot and that King Arthur had married Guinevere in this ancient capital. Malory was writing at the time of the Wars of the Roses, a troubled time that would perhaps relish the idea of a just and noble king. The Tudors, whose dynasty arose from this war and the subsequent joining together of the houses of York and Lancaster, would go on to make use of Winchester's association with Camelot.

X-rays of this painting have revealed a younger face of Arthur, thought to resemble Henry VIII in his early thirties.

Tudor Aspirations

Despite its iconic status, the Round Table was not painted until a date between 1516 and 1522. The painting shows the seated figure of King Arthur with the Tudor rose at his feet. The rose is large and positioned in the centre of the table. The face of King Arthur is thought to intentionally resemble that of Henry VIII, thus imbuing the Tudor line with a legitimacy reaching back to an ancient royal figure, one who was thought to have connections with Constantine the Great. This would have offered a diplomatic advantage when, in July 1522, Henry hosted a visit by Charles V, the Holy Roman Emperor, to Winchester's Great Hall where the newly painted Round Table was on display. In linking his family to King Arthur, Henry was following in the footsteps of his father, Henry VII. In order to consolidate the rule of the new Tudor dynasty, Henry VII brought his wife, Elizabeth of York, to Winchester to give birth to their first child, whom they named Arthur. The Tudors, with their Welsh heritage, would have wished to emphasise their Celtic connection with this historic, or legendary, figure. Henry VII's son was born in the Prior's Hall, now the Deanery, in September 1486. He was baptised on 24 September in Winchester Cathedral in a silver font brought especially from Canterbury. Prince Arthur died at the age of fifteen, leaving his brother, Henry VIII, to continue the Tudor line.

The Deanery, formerly the Prior's House, where Prince Arthur was born.

The Butterfly Bishop and King Arthur

The legend of King Arthur, 'the once and future king', includes the myth that the king lies asleep waiting for a time when he is called to arms. However, his sleep can be broken once every seven years and on these occasions he may make an unexpected appearance. One such appearance is said to have occurred in Winchester in the presence of Peter des Roches, Bishop of Winchester from 1205 to 1238. This was expedient as the bishop was not popular, and the claim that he had met King Arthur would have given him an aura of spirituality that could only have aided him in the medieval political world. England was a particularly troubled place at the time: King John was at war with the barons and the French had invaded. As adviser to the king, Peter des Roches was at the centre of events – perhaps he felt in need of a miracle. The story takes place on what has subsequently become known as Sleepers Hill, on the western outskirts of Winchester. The bishop was out hunting beyond the city walls when he became separated from his huntsmen:

> it so happened that the bishop, who was making his way over level ground, saw a beautiful new house which was hitherto unknown to him. He admired its charm, was amazed that anyone could conceive it, and hastened to take a closer look. So, as he was approaching it, there ran towards him a number of servants splendidly dressed, who hastily urged him to come at once to the feast of the king, who was expecting him; he hesitated and excused himself, saying that he had with him no dress suitable for a bishop's dinner-party. They however put on him a suitable mantle and brought him into the court to the presence of the king, who greeted him as his guest. He took his place on the right of this great prince, where there were placed before him dishes and drinks of choice quality. This however did not deter him from asking the king during the meal who he was and from whence he had come: the king declared that he was Arthur, once overlord of the whole kingdom of Britain. Peter congratulated him and asked him if he was well: 'In truth,' he replied, 'I look for God's great mercy.' The bishop then said, 'My lord, who will believe me when I say that on this day I saw or spoke to King Arthur?' The king replied 'Close your right hand,' and as he did so he continued, 'Open it': when he did so, out flew a butterfly. 'Throughout your life,' he said, 'you will have this as my memorial, that at whatever time of year you wish to see this kind of insect fly, do as you have just done and your wish will be fulfilled.' This sign later became so well known that men often asked for a butterfly as a blessing, and many used to call him the Butterfly Bishop.
>
> Peter Gallup, 'Winchester Cathedral Record Vol. 62', 1993. The story was originally taken from the *Chronicon de Lanercost* and translated from Latin by Austin Whitaker.

In October 1216 King John died and Henry III was crowned by Peter des Roches. This signalled the end of the First Barons' War and the defeat of the French. Still in a position of power, Peter des Roches went on to oversee the building of Winchester's Great Hall in 1222.

The tomb of Peter des Roches, bishop and influential figure of state, now resting in Winchester Cathedral.

The name Sleepers Hill is first recorded on a manorial plan of 1639.

Bullet Holes and the Demise of the Castle

The Round Table became a focus of anti-Royalist feeling during the Civil War of the mid-seventeenth century. This became apparent in 1976 when the table was taken down for examination. Brian Heard, Deputy Head of the Firearms Section, Metropolitan Police Forensic-Science Laboratory, New Scotland Yard, was asked to report on a number of holes that had been discovered. His report concluded that they were made by missiles and that the king's head and the Tudor rose had been the primary targets. The evidence points to this happening in 1642 when Winchester fell to Cromwell's Parliamentary force. Royalist supporters regained control of the castle, but it once again fell into Cromwell's hands in 1645. By 1651 the castle had been all but destroyed by the Parliamentarians.

The cathedral grounds, scene of religious processions and unruly disputes during the time of the Pestilence.

James, *Hampshire Papers*). The area of The Square became a point of tension between the Church and the townspeople due to the high number of burials that were necessary. The Square used to be known as Royal Palace Square due to the fact that William the Conqueror's royal palace had once stood there. From the twelfth century the people of Winchester had used this area, which lay adjacent to the Cathedral Yard, for regular markets, jousting contests, and a biannual fair. They did not want their marketplace to be encroached upon by the Church and used for the burial of plague victims. In January 1349, Ralph de Staunton, a monk of St Swithun's, was attacked whilst conducting a burial. In June 1349, townspeople, led by the mayor, 'assaulted in warlike array and with din of arms' the bishop's servants and 'the monks from the cathedral and men bearing bodies to the graveyard' (*Calendar of Patent Rolls*, 1348–50, 385). Despite this opposition from the townsfolk, many plague victims were buried in the cathedral grounds, as was discovered in the 1960s during excavation work prior to the building of the Wessex Hotel. Following the confrontations of 1349, the townspeople erected a wall between the cathedral, Great Minster Street and The Square to separate the market from the plague burial ground.

The Black Death had a devastating effect on both the population and the wealth of Winchester. The reduction of its workforce led to a decline in sources of trade and income such as the cloth-finishing industry. These social and economic problems were compounded when plague returned in 1361 and again in the 1370s. By 1452 there were 997 empty houses and seventeen churches without priests. Much of the west and north of the city became derelict or was turned into pasture, and these areas were not built on until the population recovered in the nineteenth century.

The high death toll amongst the clergy resulted in Bishop Wykeham founding Winchester College.

Winchester's clergy suffered in great numbers during the plague years – church records show 48 per cent mortality. This led to the closure and abandonment of many parish churches within the city. In 1366, the talented and ambitious William of Wykeham succeeded Edington as Bishop of Winchester. Wykeham's solution to the depleted numbers of clergymen was to build two new colleges dedicated to the education of boys and young men. In 1379, Wykeham established the 'College of St Mary of Winchester at Oxford', which became known as New College, Oxford. Three years later, in 1382, he founded 'the College of St Mary of Winchester', now known as Winchester College. The founding purpose of Winchester College was to educate seventy 'poor and needy scholars' who would then go on to complete a theological education at New College. Both of these institutions, founded as a result of the Black Death, are still thriving today.

The Great Plague

Various forms of plague returned after 1350. In all it is believed that there were three types of plague: bubonic, septicaemic and pneumonic. In 1625, a severe outbreak of plague took place, but it was in 1665 that it once again took hold in the form of the Great Plague. By this time it was understood that disease spread through some form of contact, which led to many plague victims being shut away in their homes to die. Whole families were known to have perished in this way, including John Jerome, a craftsman and cathedral painter who died along with his wife and children in St Maurice's parish.

The beauty spot of Plague Pit Valley lies at the foot of St Catherine's Hill.

Winchester's Plague Monument. Part of the inscription reads, 'the City lay under the Scourge of the Destroying Pestilence'.

In 1665 and 1667, to prevent the spread of disease Winchester College was shut and the boys sent to the village of Crawley. Once again, the need for a place to bury the dead became an issue. This time a decision was made to use an area outside the city walls, just south of St Catherine's Hill. This area, between St Catherine's Hill and Twyford Down, is now known as 'Plague Pit Valley'.

The Plague Monument, erected in 1759 just outside the city's West Gate, marks the spot where goods were exchanged for money during the time of earlier plagues. As a precaution against infection, traders would bring their produce to this point just outside the city; the townsfolk would keep their distance and pay for the goods by leaving coins in a bowl of vinegar. Following the Great Plague, the Charitable Society of Natives and Citizens was formed with the aim of helping the orphaned children of Winchester by providing education and apprenticeships. It was later joined by the Society of Aliens in 1720 (for residents not born in the city). Together the societies funded the monument.

Eighteenth-Century Bones

In the 1830s, when digging a cutting for the new railway line, workers discovered a plethora of skeletons and skulls buried in the shadow of the old King's House. The King's House was the only completed part of a palace, designed by Sir Christopher Wren for Charles II, intended to be on a similar scale to Versailles. Upon the king's death in 1685 the building was left unfinished. It stood in the same position as the old castle and was, by the 1800s, being used as a military establishment. The area eventually became known as the Peninsula Barracks. In the 1990s, when the lower part of this area was developed for residential housing, many more skeletons were discovered. Where had all these bones come from? For much of the latter part of the eighteenth century the King's House

The King's House as it was in the early 1800s. The area is now known as Peninsula Barracks.

had become a widespread practice which threatened the value of the national currency. In 1278, large numbers of people, both Christians and Jews, were accused of this offence, rounded up and sent to the Tower of London. Benedict was one of around 680 Jews detained in the Tower. Despite his connections with Winchester's wealthy citizens, Benedict became one of the 269 Jews hanged for coin clipping, late in 1278–79. Following his execution, the Crown sized all of Benedict's goods and property; the list of possessions included 124 gold rings and 105 garnets. His total property in Winchester was sold for £207 7s 8d. In all, the Treasury gained at least £10,000 from confiscated property at this time. It is thought that Benedict was buried by the medieval gaol that lay between Jewry Street and Staple Gardens.

The Jewish Cemetery

Winchester's medieval Jewish cemetery lay just outside the city walls on the western side of the castle. It was created on a plot of land rented from the Priory of St Swithun's following permission granted in 1177 by King Henry II for cemeteries to be established outside of London. Prior to this date bereaved Jews were expected to travel to London to bury their dead. Excavation of the cemetery in 1974–75 and 1995 revealed that many suffered from rickets, a symptom of poverty and subsequent malnourishment, demonstrating that there were many poor Jews living alongside the wealthy families such as Licoricia's. The skull of one unfortunate man was found to have two wounds inflicted by either an axe or a sword.

The Cathedral

In the 1960s, wall paintings believed to date from around 1160 were discovered behind plasterwork in the Holy Sepulchre Chapel of Winchester Cathedral. These paintings

Twelfth-century wall paintings uncovered in Winchester Cathedral.

include medieval depictions of Jewish men, identifiable by their distinctive hats. There is one image that is thought to represent Joseph of Arimathea. He is shown washing Jesus following the crucifixion and is depicted wearing a traditional conical hat. Inside Bishop Stephen Gardiner's chantry chapel is a stone carving of Synagogia, which dates from around 1558. Synagogia, who can be identified by her blindfold, represents both the Christian Old Testament and the Jewish religion. Traditionally she is shown alongside Ecclesia who represents the Christian faith. Unfortunately, a thirteenth-century statue believed to be of Ecclesia has suffered severe damage and is not reliably identifiable, but can still be seen in the retrochoir of the cathedral.

A sixteenth-century representation of Synagogia inside Bishop Gardiner's Chantry Chapel.

The Great Hall where many trials and court hearings took place. This gathering – note the wigged gentleman – dates from around the 1830s.

Revolting Winchester

After the Black Death of the 1340s, when a third of Europe's population was decimated, there was a drastic shortage of people to work the land. Labourers began to recognise their value and demanded higher wages and better working conditions, which eventually led to the Peasants' Revolt of 1381 across large parts of the country. This major uprising was also fuelled by an increase in taxes as a result of conflict with France during the Hundred Years' War. Rebels demanded better working conditions and an end to unfree labour, known as serfdom, and sought to remove the king's senior officials.

In Winchester, the unease seems to have been centred on the way old legal practices flowing from royal authority was damaging trade. The rebels were mainly from the woollen cloth trade, many with civic standing, and they were led by William Wygge, a wealthy draper. He was also a senior member of the Merchant's Guild, and resented the Staple's independent administration of commercial contracts and debts involving their members. Winchester was one of ten Staple towns that had been established in 1353. A 'Staple' was a place or port where commodities – wool in Winchester's case – were brought, weighed and customs paid before they were sold or exported. They also had their own court, which handled any disputes over commercial matters.

In June of 1381 news of more uprisings in Surrey and London reached Winchester and this was the excuse Wygge and his rebels needed. They gathered support by ringing the town bell and blowing the moot horn. The following day they broke into the King's Staple, stole all the rolls and records stored there and burned them in the High Street. A Walter Hogyn, believed to be the Staple clerk, was killed.

Interestingly, at the London Smithfield showdown between the fourteen-year-old Richard II and Wat Tyler, who swills and spits ale in front of his king, the Peasants' Revolt leader demands a return to 'the Law of Winchester'. This referred to the Statute of Winchester of 1285 that allowed communities to look after their own law enforcement.

Centuries on, there were several showdowns between other members of the city's society; namely Winchester College commoners and townsmen. James Harris, the first Earl of Malmesbury, who had been educated at Winchester, received several letters from his mother describing these 'Town vs Gown' riots:

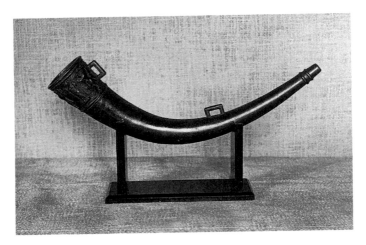

Left: The Moot Horn is now on display in the City Museum; recent study shows it dates from the twelfth century.

Below: The area of Staple Gardens, once a major trading centre for wool merchants.

Salisbury March 3, 1770

The riot I mentioned in my last, at Winchester, is all over and no one expelled. It is a formidable thing, for they had several brace of pistols. It began, as I hear, by the landlord of the White Hart desiring some of the commoners who were drinking at his house, not to drink any more, but to go home; this gave such offence, that the next day some went and broke his windows, the man was obliged to call his neighbours to his assistance, so that brought on the battle between the townsmen and the scholars. The great hero's name is Hare, he had been expelled from Eton.

Several years later, in 1793, there would be another riot, this rebellion at a time when the spirit of the French Revolution was in the air. The boys were confined closely to the school premises, so when one prefect slipped out to hear the Band of the Bucks Militia in Cathedral Close, all hell broke loose. The warden, George Huntingford, decided to punish him by depriving the whole school of Easter leave, whereby the boys seized keys from the porter, locked up the warden and prepared for a siege. The Red Cap of Liberty was raised to the top of the main gate and stones on the parapet were loosened. The High Sheriff was called and calm was eventually restored.

Another eighteenth-century riot centred around the Buttercross, or City Cross, which was destined for a wealthy landowner's garden. The century had seen the destruction of

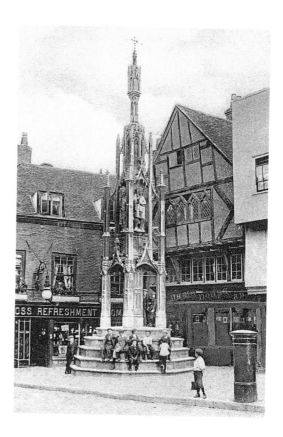

The City Cross, or Buttercross, being enjoyed by a group of schoolboys at the turn of the twentieth century.

many buildings and the city's medieval past neglected, but when the Corporation intended to sell the stone cross to Mr Dummer of Cranbury Park, feisty residents protested. An angry demonstration took place and the much-loved local landmark on the High Street remained. Mr Dummer would be without his Gothic ornament.

DID YOU KNOW ?

In Cromwell's time, the bell of St Lawrence's Church would be tolled before public executions that took place in The Square. The last time would probably have been in 1685 at the execution of Dame Alice Lisle. In Elizabeth I's reign the bell was used temporarily as the city's curfew bell.

DID YOU KNOW ?

A Russian Gun, captured in the Crimean War and presented to the city, once stood in the Broadway. The area around it had become popular, a sort of 'Speaker's corner', and so when the railings were removed during preparations for the 1908 National Pageant, civic unrest ensued. In what became known as the 'Gun Riots', over 3,000 people gathered, led by local house painter Joe Dumper. Joe restored peace the next day, after the railings were reinstalled. They and the gun were to remain until 1939 when they were scrapped to aid the war effort.

The area around the Russian Gun in the Broadway became a popular meeting place.

8. Churches and Chapels

The Soke

It is from a viewpoint on St Giles Hill that we can appreciate Winchester's architectural heritage, and amongst the buildings pick out the spires of churches and chapels, and ancient stonework of the cathedral and palace. It is hard to imagine how, at the turn of the thirteenth century, the many ecclesiastical buildings must have completely dominated the landscape, as at that time there stood the cathedral priory, two abbeys, four friaries, four non-parochial chapels, and no less than fifty-four parish churches.

It is not just buildings however, that are evidence of how religion has shaped Winchester's history and landscape, but the land as well. In 1096 William Rufus granted an annual fair to Bishop Wakelin who needed to finance the cost of building the new cathedral. It was the first charter of its kind issued since the Norman Conquest and the gift gave the bishop and the monks of the cathedral priory all rents that were paid during the period of the fair, which was held on St Giles Hill. The success of St Giles fair, which became one of the most important in Europe, resulted in it being extended from three days to sixteen days in 1155, and the bishop's control over it indicated the power of the Church at that time. There was a courthouse on St Giles Hill known as Pavilion Hall,

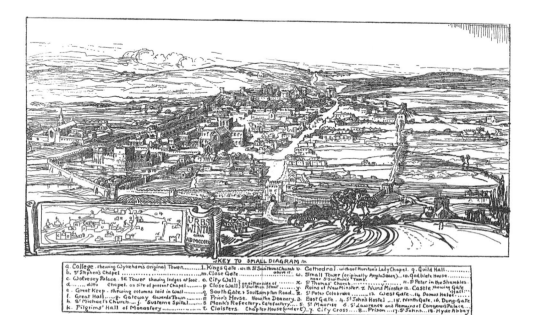

How the city may have looked in 1450. This artist's impression was published in 1913.

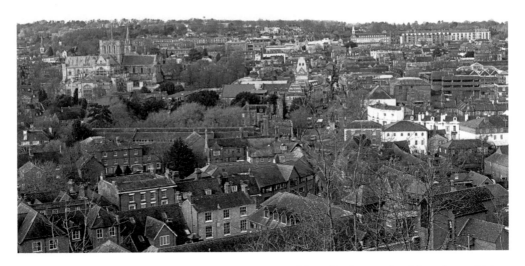

The view from St Giles Hill today. During the medieval fair all other trade taking place within a 10-mile radius had to cease.

an administrative centre that managed the fair; late thirteenth- and fourteenth-century records indicate many staff including a justiciar, a chamberlain, a marshal, gatekeeper and several armed sergeants who guarded it day and night. By the sixteenth century the name had changed to Palm Hall, and as justice was given out, it became known as Palm Court – today there is a Palm Court Close near to its original site.

In 1231, 'The Soke', as it is still referred to, was created by Bishop Peter des Roches, also known as the Butterfly Bishop (*see chapter four*). This was to be the bishop's estate: land to the east and south outside the city walls, including St Giles Hill, and from then on Winchester was divided into two jurisdictions answering to the king and bishop, respectively. The 'Bishop's Soke' reflected the importance and high status of the bishop, and was represented by a bailiff and held its own court, which became known as Cheyney Court. The Soke prison at Wolvesey Palace was later located on St John's Street. It was known as Cheyney Court prison and had stocks nearby.

College of St Elizabeth of Hungary

Across from the Bishops' Palace in an area once known as St Stephen's Mead, and to the south-east of where Winchester College would come to be established, once stood the College of St Elizabeth of Hungary. It was founded in 1301 by Bishop John de Pontissara and was a Chantry College with a substantial church and belfry, and where the community of secular priests would pray for the souls of the deceased, particularly those of the royal family and the bishops of Winchester. In addition to priests, the college also consisted of a warden, six clerks or students and six choristers. It survived until the Reformation when it was dissolved, and in 1544 the warden and fellows of Winchester College purchased it for £350. Their intention was to use it as a boarding house for commoners, but another building on College Street was used instead, and St Elizabeth of Hungary was demolished in 1547.

The meadow upon which the College of St Elizabeth of Hungary was once situated. New Hall of Winchester College is on the right.

St Mary Kalendar and the Symonds Family

St Elizabeth's was one of the many ecclesiastical buildings that would not survive the Reformation; many others would be destroyed or fall into decline. St Mary Kalendar once stood on the site of Nos 118–120 High Street, opposite the eastern end of the Pentice, and took its name from the small college of Kalendar monks that served it. They had a close association with the bishop and it was here that a new bishop was welcomed before his enthronement ceremony at the cathedral – this privilege was later to move to St Lawrence's Church in The Square. Due to its central location St Mary was a principal parish church and one of the largest and wealthiest. The fraternity was dissolved as a chantry in 1547–53, when it was described as a college, and by 1640 the parsonage was still in existence, but the church in ruins. Excavations took place in 1929 during the construction of Woolworth's and remains of the monk's cells were found on the northern side, and floors of encaustic and marble tiles were found on the site of the church.

St Mary Kalendar was the family church of the Symonds family. In around 1528, Peter Symonds was born into this wealthy and well-established Protestant family, when the Pope was still head of the Church in England. He was therefore to live through a period of remarkable religious change, which saw not only the Reformation, but after Edward VI's short reign, the equally short-lived reign of Queen Mary, who sought to return Catholicism to the country. Symonds had left for London in around 1543 to become an apprentice to a London mercer, William Wilkinson; his company imported cotton and linen goods from Germany and Flanders and exported English cloth. Living in an evangelical household he would not have welcomed the news, several years later, of the marriage of Mary to Philip of Spain, which was held in Winchester Cathedral.

As a puritan Protestant, Peter had been keen on preaching and made bequests in his will to encourage this, financing an Easter sermon at the church of St Mary Kalendar. He also

Left: Stones from the ruins of Hyde Abbey can be seen in the chimney stacks of Christ's Hospital on Symonds Street.

Below: Still standing. The Hyde Abbey Gatehouse survived the Dissolution of the Monasteries.

made provision for bread doles for the poor in London and also at the cathedral and St Mary Kalendar. Although Symonds wealth was later used to establish Peter Symonds' School, his greatest charitable bequest was Christ's Hospital on Symonds Street; these almshouses became home to 'six poor men and four poor boys'. It was founded in 1607, and 100 carts of stone from the ruins of the dissolved Hyde Abbey were brought across the city and used in the foundations and in the base of the walls and chimney stacks.

DID YOU KNOW ?

St Swithun upon Kingsgate features in Anthony Trollope's novel *The Warden*, when Warden Harding becomes rector of 'St Cuthbert's' after resigning from Hiram's Hospital, which is usually identified with the Hospital of St Cross. Trollope's memories of schooldays at Winchester College are likely to have played a part in his conception of Barchester:

> The church is a singular little Gothic building, perched over a gateway, through which the Close is entered, and is approached by a flight of stone steps which leads down under the archway of the gate. It is no bigger than an ordinary room – perhaps twenty-seven feet long by eighteen wide – but still it is a perfect church... (Chapter 21)

St James Cemetery: last resting place of many persecuted Catholics in the sixteenth and seventeenth centuries.

9. What Did the Victorians Do for Us?

The nineteenth century was one of growth and development; the Industrial Revolution had made Britain a world leader in the production of iron, steel and steam engines, and the cotton and woollen mills boomed, which increased international trade. It was a century that saw great municipal work such as the construction of sewers, which halted epidemics of cholera and typhoid. There were many achievements in science, medicine and the arts, and the work of the first pioneers in photography was being marvelled at and enjoyed. There was a tremendous feeling of national pride and progress and this was celebrated in the Great Exhibition of 1851.

During this century, the population of Winchester almost tripled. In the 1801 census, it stood at 5,826 and had reached 17,179 by 1891. The census of 1851, eleven years after the railway had arrived in Winchester from London, recorded a considerable number of men, women and children who were not born here. The Southampton–Winchester line had opened a year earlier, in 1839. Many of these new arrivals contributed to the economic progress of the city and many dedicated themselves to the welfare of its citizens.

Victorian letter box on Kingsgate Street

DID YOU KNOW ?

A refurbished Sewer Gas Destructor Lamp stands on Great Minster Street. This lantern was patented in 1895 by J. E. Webb of Birmingham. Its purpose was to enable gases from the sewer below to escape, preventing a potentially hazardous build-up. The gas then reached a burner at the top of the lantern where it would ignite, providing constant street illumination.

Putting gases to good use.

Street Scenes

Thomas Stopher, an architect from Saxmundham in Suffolk, came to Winchester as a county surveyor in 1841. His son, also called Thomas and also an architect, was responsible for many impressive brick and timber buildings still visible today. They were often on corner sites such as the Talbot Inn on the corner of High Street and Staple Gardens, the Dolphin Inn on the High Street and St Thomas Street, and The Green Man on Southgate Street and St Swithun Street. The impressive De Lunn Buildings on Jewry Street, with their steeply pitched roofs, was another of his designs.

Thomas Stopher Junior went on to become alderman and mayor, and was involved with the redevelopment of St Giles Hill, both in his civic role and that of an architect. Financial reform of the mid-nineteenth century meant it was now possible to sell off land belonging to the bishop and in 1878 the Corporation bought the 'front' of the hill (facing the city) for £1,250. They received the area sloping down to Magdalen Hill Road as a gift and work began on creating a wooded 'pleasure ground' area. He had already been involved in the design of many of the large homes on the hill.

Stopher was concerned that the city would change considerably in the twentieth century, so he commissioned local artist Beatrice Olive Corfe to paint views of Winchester so that many of the buildings would be recorded. Beatrice was born in Winchester in 1866 and lived with her parents and seven siblings in Kingsgate Street, later moving to Chesil Street. Images of nearby Bridge Street and Wharf Hill were two of the watercolours Beatrice produced. Four drawings recording the interior of the Canon's house in Cathedral Close are held in the Victoria & Albert Museum collection. Beatrice was also a skilled botanical artist and in the 1930s the Natural History Museum commissioned her to paint some watercolours, which were then reproduced as postcards. After the Second World War her collection of plant watercolours and sketchbook were bequeathed to the museum, where they are still held. She died in Winchester in 1947.

One of several pub buildings designed by Thomas Stopher. Built in 1882, this was the Dolphin Inn.

The Tourist Trade

Needlework was a popular Victorian pastime and it was materials for this craft that William Savage and his wife Mary began selling from their shop at No. 12 The Square, and where, in 1836, they also established a warehouse. The arrival of the railway saw a huge increase in visitors to the city, and their business soon developed into a trade in souvenirs – the shop being in an ideal location, catching tourists on their way to the cathedral. Savage began to sell a collection of 'Winchester' china – items decorated with local scenes applied by transfer. Along with Copeland-Spode, a variety of items were produced – cups, saucers, plates, vases and teapots – all decorated in colour with local scenes such as the cathedral, St Cross, Winchester College and its 'Trusty Servant'. By 1858 William and Mary had moved premises to No. 97 High Street; the shop was referred to in an advert of 1868 as 'The Depot of City Memorials'.

Alongside the souvenir china, William also contributed to the tourist trade as a publisher, promoting Winchester through his guides and publications. However, it is as a photographer that he is possibly best remembered, working from his studio in St Michaels Road, known as the 'Wykeham Studio', and from the rear of the shop. Between 1865 and 1900 he produced a collection of photographs of the city and surrounding views, and also

An advert for William and Mary's shop with a selection of their souvenir china.

Photograph taken by William Savage to illustrate *The Hospital of St Cross,* a book published by him in 1868.

many portraits of local people and dignitaries in the form of carte-de-visite, or visiting cards. With processes becoming simpler and cheaper, the photograph grew ever more popular. These carte-de-visite were normal visiting cards but with a portrait of the person on the back, and because they were cheap, most people could afford to have portraits of themselves and their families on display.

The Museum Age
In 1845 the Museums Act was introduced, which was to encourage the establishment of museums in large towns. In the same year the British Archaeological Association and the Archaeological Institute both held meetings in Winchester and the *London Illustrated News* reported on the latter saying, 'the room was crowded with fashionable company, among whom were many ladies'. An increase in both academic and public interest in the city's history and antiquities led to a proposal to found a museum, and at the Corn Exchange in October 1846 a meeting was held and a resolution passed to the effect that it was 'highly desirable a general public museum for the county should be established in the city of Winchester'.

Donations and subscriptions were asked for, and on 15 July (St Swithun's Day) 1847, the museum was opened in the former Hyde Abbey School House on Hyde Street. The first item acquired was a Roman urn that had been excavated during digging for the foundations of a gasholder in Water Lane. The museum began as a county venture and was initially known as 'The Hampshire Museum', but in 1851 it became the City Museum,

The former Hyde Abbey School House, home to the first county museum.

a year in which there were 2,000 visitors. Henry Moody was the enthusiastic first curator. He began in 1847 and moved with the museum in 1851 to the vacant house of the governor of the old gaol on Jewry Street, and soon after, in 1853, he compiled its first catalogue, and completed a second one in 1858. It was open to the public three days a week and had on display 'casts of Hampshire seals, rubbings of brasses, and other archaeological remains from the city and county, and a small collection of stuffed birds and other animals'.

Moody gave lectures on many subjects and wrote numerous books and articles, which were invaluable for their references to Winchester, and records of memories of older people he had known. He resigned as curator in 1871, apparently having sold off certain items from the museum without permission. Three years later the collection went on to be housed at the top of the new Guildhall, which had recently been completed. In 1883, Moody's daughter was acting as a guide for the collection and was reportedly heard saying to a visitor that her father had 'half ruined himself by publishing archaeological works, but she was not sorry for it'. In 1903 the City Museum moved to its current location in The Square. It was the first purpose-built museum outside London.

A Portsmouth Grocer

As the population of Winchester continued to grow, many epitomised the spirit of the Victorian age and became quite the entrepreneur. Charles Witman Benny was one such person. Born in 1794, he was originally a grocer from Portsmouth who bought his first shop on Winchester High Street in 1820. He was also active in local politics and became mayor in 1834.

In the 1830s the graveyards of Winchester's churches were becoming overcrowded and there was no cemetery, but this all changed in 1839 when Benny formed the Winchester Cemetery Company with capital of £5,000. Construction of the cemetery began on the south side of what was Barnes Lane, now St James Lane, on the slope of West Hill. Two chapels and a gate lodge were designed by architect Owen Brown Carter, who had recently built the Corn Exchange on Jewry Street. The chapels were demolished in the 1930s but the lodge still stands. The company was incorporated by an Act of Parliament, which stated the charges for interments: for every person buried in the open ground the sum of twelve shillings; for every person buried in a purchased or private grave the sum of two guineas; and for every person buried in a vault, catacomb or brick grave the sum of four guineas. Mr Benny took a keen interest in the running of the cemetery, and it is said that he insisted the keeper who lived at the lodge have a large dog to protect the graves of recently buried people from grave robbers.

Benny's next big venture was forming the Winchester Waterworks Company, which would provide piped water to many establishments. A well of 200 feet deep, not far from his cemetery on West Hill, held a sufficient supply and two steam engines were deployed to raise and distribute the water. He retired from civil life in 1853, but six years later opened a new hotel, The Royal, on St Peters Street, the premises having been vacated by the Benedictine nuns two years earlier. This new hotel was under the management of The White Hart inn's ex-landlord, a shrewd move of Benny's as The White Hart, which had closed in 1857, had been one of Winchester's most famous inns. Coaching inns such as The White Hart continued to offer a road service to visitors and

Gothic memorials within West Hill Cemetery; the Gate Lodge can be seen on the left.

10. Trains, Planes and Automobiles

The Didcot, Newbury and Southampton Railway

The 'railway mania' of the 1840s saw many proposals for new lines across the country. Of these there were several companies whose intentions were to provide a North–South link between the Midlands and the south coast, or more importantly, Southampton. It was an indication of how the port was developing commercially. Many schemes never got off the ground, but as the network grew, plans were revived and in 1873 a parliamentary bill was submitted for the construction of the Didcot, Newbury and Southampton Railway.

The newly formed DN&SR company, operated by the Great Western Railway, completed the line between Newbury and Winchester in 1885 (Didcot to Newbury was completed three years earlier) and opened the new station on the east side of the city. The line only reached as far as Bar End, where the goods yard was located, as the company had run into financial difficulty and was forced into a compromise with the operator of the main line from London to Southampton – the London and South Western Railway (L&SWR). In 1891, the L&SWR provided a connection on to the main line at Shawford, thereby halting DN&SR's aim for an independent route all the way to the major port of Southampton. This meant that the unfortunate passengers had to

Winchester 'Cheesehill' station in the 1960s.

wait in their carriages at the station whilst the GWR engine was uncoupled, driven clear to make way for a waiting L&SWR engine to reverse up and couple up. The passengers were then able to resume the remainder of their journey, skirting around the water meadows and over the Hockley Viaduct, joining the main line to Southampton at Shawford Junction.

'Winchester Cheesehill', as it was first named, was the largest and most important station on the new DN&SR line, which came to be referred to as 'Dirty, Noisy and Slow'! It warranted a higher grade of stationmaster and records show that around fifteen members of staff were employed there, more than at the L&SWR station on the west side of town. Many were responsible for the engine-changing manoeuvres, but there were also clerks, foremen, guards, drivers, porters, warehousemen, firemen and cleaners. There was even a station cat, who apparently sported the correct attire.

Walking around the Chesil Street area now, it would be easy to miss the signs that a busy station once existed here. The former stationmaster's house can be seen from the path leading up St Giles Hill, his garden a narrow strip of lawn situated over the former line, just above the entrance to the tunnel. The path carries on along the top of what was the railway cutting until the footbridge is reached, where GWR broad gauge ties can be seen at regular intervals within the fencing. These are a reminder of the presence of the company in what was considered L&SWR territory. Also marking the

The former stationmaster's house.

This footbridge takes you from the original railway cutting on St Giles Hill, over the former railway line and down to Chesil Street.

boundary between the two rival railway companies are the colours of the footbridge that leads back down to street level, which is painted in cream and brown (GWR) and green (L&SWR).

The railway tunnel hidden beneath St Giles Hill is a quarter of a mile long (around 400 metres). When it was being excavated, the length proved contentious, as to qualify for extra pay in the form of a tunnel allowance, the track gangs had to reach 440 yards (the official length for a tunnel). Initially the measurement was 439 yards but as the tunnel curved, this was appealed and the longer side was measured. This was 441 yards, so the gangs got their allowance. It was partially relined and reinforced in the 1920s and '30s, but was always damp with the sound of dripping water throughout. A task of one of the gangers would be to walk through the tunnel and knock off the icicles from the roof, some of which were said to be up to 6 feet in length. The entrance is still visible near to the Chesil Street multistorey car park, and periodically there are guided tours where you are able to walk the entire length of the (still damp!) tunnel. The space is used by Winchester City Council for storage purposes.

The quarter-mile tunnel under St Giles Hill provides a useful storage facility for the city.

Traffic at the railway's goods shed was mainly coal but also a considerable amount of livestock, mainly cattle for the October Fair, which was held in what is now the King George V playing fields, on Bar End Road. Cattle were herded from these fields, across the road, and into the goods yard where they were loaded through the pens. Before the Second World War, up to twenty-five wagons arrived or departed at a time. There were also two sheep auctions a year, held in the same fields and often, due to unskilled labour unused to herding the animals, they escaped all over the yard causing much chaos. After the war, roads replaced rail for the movement of livestock, and the area was used mainly for coal traffic during the railway's final years. One of the many coal merchants in the area was a Messrs G. W. Piper, a business that started in 1897 and continued until 1964. A siding to the west of the line was used for the coal wagons that provided steam coal for the nearby Domum Laundry.

There were also deliveries by rail of fish, groceries and general merchandise for the city's businesses. Boots the Chemist had one or two wagons a week and in the 1950s Marks & Spencer had a contract for deliveries, particularly crumpets, whilst from Reading came a regular delivery of Huntley & Palmers biscuits, which was then distributed around Winchester by their own vehicle.

DID YOU KNOW ?

Between the former goods yard of Bar End and Wharf Hill is a field once used as a 'tenter ground'. Here cloth was hung out on wooden framed tenters to prevent shrinkage as it dried, tenterhooks holding the cloth in place. Tenters were used as far back as the fourteenth century, but it was in the mid-eighteenth century that 'on tenterhooks' became an expression of uneasiness or tension.

In the mid-sixteenth century this field was known as Puttockspark, or Rackhill.

DID YOU KNOW ?

On Twyford Down a series of parallel hollows known as Dongas, the Matabele word for a gully, can be seen. These were ancient trackways formed from the herding of animals over many centuries. In the early 1990s the construction of the M3 motorway cutting through the Down severed the Dongas from St Catherine's Hill. A group of travellers living near to the Dongas, and protesting against the work, were given the name 'The Dongas Tribe'.

The Prince and Princess of Wales at the Royal Agricultural Show at Bar End, 1883.

Preaching to the Navvies

The Evangelical church in Highcliffe started life as the Royal Pavilion for the Prince and Princess of Wales, who attended the Royal Counties Agricultural Show in 1883. After this event, two local ladies, Misses Clark, bought the corrugated iron building and had it moved to plot 14 in St Catherine's Road. This was on the new development of the Highcliffe Estate, an area of housing built as a result of the growth of the city in the latter half of nineteenth century. Pyotts field, on the eastern slope of Winchester, was deemed ideal and promoted as 'some of the best situated building sites in the city' with 'good drainage, pure water, elevated, bracing and salubrious position, magnificent views'.

Another factor in the siting of the Highcliffe Estate was the location of the new railway line, the construction of which brought large numbers of navvies to the area whom the two ladies, Misses Clark, were keen to preach to in their newly situated church. After the completion of the railway, the mission hall continued to be used as a Brethren Assembly, and in 1930 it became the Evangelical Church.

The Railway in Wartime

During the First World War, three large military camps were set up on the downs north-east of the city. The furthest was almost in the estate of Avington Park; the other two were on Winnall Down and Morn Hill. Americans, Canadians, Australians, New Zealanders and South Africans as well as British servicemen were all stationed here. Morn Hill alone could accommodate in the region of 50,000 men and it became the largest concentration in Britain of troops in transit to the Western Front. At this time the population of Winchester was only around 20,000..

Military life at one of the camps on Winnall Down.

The US Government paid for a camp line to be built and the work was carried out by the Royal Engineers with the help of American soldiers and ex-servicemen straight out of war duty. It diverted away from the main railway line around a third of a mile from the Chesil Station, just north of the tunnel. It cut across the Winnall area, which at this time was open countryside, and climbed up across the downs to a point where a siding led to the former isolation hospital at Magdalen Hill. (This was the Victoria Hospital that had been built in 1887 for Winchester City Council, which managed it until 1948.) It had been converted to military use and was equipped with operating theatres. The route then turned north-east towards Winnall Down Farm, over a crossing at Easton Road and across to the terminus at Avington Park Camp, 3 miles from the junction.

It was not used as a troop train but for deliveries of supplies such as coal and large quantities of flour to the Winnall Down camp where a bakery had been established. It is possible, however, that some ambulance trains may have reached the hospital siding. The railway remained in use until the camps were closed in 1920 and the track remained until 1923, which was when the DN&SR became property of the GWR.

During the Second World War the DN&SR once again provided an important transport link to the south coast, especially in the run-up to D-Day, when the efficient movement of troops and supplies was crucial. The line operated for almost seventy-five years; the staff at Chesil Station saw their last passenger train in 1960, although freight continued for a further six years.

Sausages, Onions and Potatoes

The founder of King Alfred Motor Services, Robert Chisnell, first became involved in passenger transport as a result of his workhorses being commandeered for the army. Needing transport to keep his businesses trading, he had a delivery van body built and mounted onto a Darracq chassis. He acquired more vehicles and when troops were camped at Winnall Down, he saw yet another business opportunity (*see* Pastimes and Leisure for the others). This new business became known as 'S.P.O.', which stood for sausages, potatoes and onions. The first outlet for this fare was on Bridge Street, but soon another opened on the corner of St Clement Street and St Thomas Street. Mr Chisnell then realised that he needed to transport the troops to the eateries from the camps, and so his ever-growing fleet of vehicles provided this service. The fare was said to be one shilling each way and to help overcrowding and ease the potential for boisterous behaviour on the way back up to the camps, a basic ticket system was put in place. On arrival in Bridge Street the soldiers would collect a ticket from Mr Chisnell's daughter Evelyn, at the back of the family tobacconist shop, which would state the time of their return journey.

At the end of the war, Leyland Motors began to recondition large numbers of their trucks that had seen service with the RAF, and sell them for non-military uses, usually just as a chassis. Mr Chisnell bought two such vehicles that had been fitted with charabanc bodies. The first of these was ready for its first outing on Whit Monday, 24 May 1920,

The road to the camps. The building next to the Rising Sun pub was Mr Chisnell's tobacconist shop where he also sold 'bus' tickets to the soldiers.

First charabanc outing to Bournemouth in May 1920 and the start of the King Alfred Motor Services. Founder Robert Chisnell is standing on the right wearing a cloth cap.

when its passengers headed off to Bournemouth for a day trip. This was the official start of the King Alfred Motor Service Company, which was registered as such in 1929. The buses ran services in and around the Winchester area for a further forty-four years, when it then passed to the National Bus Company.

Tanks and a Tomahawk

Opening on 1 February 1940, the A33 Winchester Bypass was one of the first fully dual carriageways in the country and thereby an important piece of road engineering in the pre-motorway era. It was agreed that it should lie east of the city, and the south-east section followed the course of the DN&S railway line, around the base of St Catherine's Hill. It was originally planned as a single-carriageway bypass, but after a small amount of work in 1931, the project was abandoned and later redesigned in 1934 as a dual carriageway. Progress was delayed with the onset of the Second World War, but by late 1939 one carriageway was being used for military traffic, and like the nearby railway, provided an important transport link for D-Day preparations. In 1944 it was used as a tank park.

Constructed in the immediate pre-war period, the Spitfire Bridge also opened in 1940 and carried the Alresford Road (A31) over the Winchester Bypass. It was a year later when George Rogers flew his Curtiss Tomahawk beneath the bridge, but experienced a near-miss with an oncoming HGV. He clipped the bridge, lost 3 feet of his plane, which caused him to crash on landing, but fortunately he walked away with only minor injuries. The story spread but no one actually knew what type of plane had flown under the bridge, and it was assumed that only a Spitfire would attempt such a manoeuvre, and so the name stuck. The bridge was demolished when the M3 replaced the bypass and the cutting was widened to house the parallel A272, which was nicknamed 'Spitfire Link'. The junction of Spitfire Link and the A31 is known as the Spitfire Roundabout.

Churchill Mk IV tanks in storage on the Winchester bypass in readiness for the invasion of Europe, 16 May 1944.

Bibliography

Ball, Charles, *An Historic Account of Winchester with Descriptive Walks* (James Robbins – College Street, 1818)

Bartlet, Suzanne, *Licoricia of Winchester* (Vallentine Mitchell & Co. Ltd, 2009)

Beaumont James, Tom, *Book of Winchester* (Batsford/English Heritage, 1997)

Beaumont James, Tom, *Hampshire Papers: The Black Death in Hampshire* (Hampshire County Council, 1999)

Biddle, Martin, and Keene, Derek, *Winchester – British Historic Towns Atlas* (The Historic Towns Trust and The Winchester Excavations Committee, 2017)

Biddle, M., & Badham, S., et al., *King Arthur's Round Table: An Archaeological Investigation (Boydell, 2000)*

Bryan, D., Buchanan, G., Dixon, C., & King, J., *Bloody British History: Winchester* (The History Press, 2013)

Carpenter Turner, Barbara, *A History of Winchester* (Phillimore, 1992)

Castor, Helen, *She-Wolves* (Faber and Faber, 2010)

Freeman, J. D. F., Jowitt, Robert, E., Murphy, R. J., *King Alfred Motor Services* (Kingfisher Railway Productions, 1984)

Gallup, Peter, *Winchester Cathedral Record Vol. 62*, 1993

Groombridge, Garth, and Kinnaird, Kirsty, *Winchester in 50 Buildings* (Amberley Publishing, 2018)

Hilliam, David, *Winchester Curiosities* (The History Press, 2011)

Hilton, Lisa, *Queens Consort* (London, Weidenfeld & Nicolson, 2008)

Himsworth, Sheila, *The Marriage of Philip II of Spain with Mary Tudor* (Proceedings of the Hampshire Field Club, Vol. XXII, Part II, 1962)

Karau, Paul, Parson, Mike, Robertson, Kevin, *The Didcot Newbury and Southampton Railway* (Wild Swan Publications Ltd, 1981)

Keene, Derek, Survey of Medieval Winchester Part 1 – Winchester Studies 2 (Clarendon Press, 1985)

Locke, A. Audrey (ed.), *In Praise of Winchester* (Constable & Co., 1912)

Ranger, Paul, *The Lost Theatres of Winchester, 1620-1861* (Hampshire Field Club Proceedings Vol 31, 1974)

Shurlock, Barry, *The Winchester Story* (Milestone Publications, 1986)

Scobie, G. and Qualmann, K., *Nunnaminster* (Winchester Museums Service, 1993)

St John Parker, Michael, *King Arthur* (Pitkin Publishing, 1995)

Thorn Warren, William, *Winchester Illustrated* (Warren's Library, 1903)

Woodward, B. B., *A History of Winchester* (1860; facsimile ed. Laurence Oxley, 1974)

Yates, Phil, *Time Gentlemen, Please!* (City of Winchester Trust, 2007)

Websites:

www.winchester.ac.uk/MJW

www.oxfordjewishheritage.co.uk

www.hiwwt.org.uk

www.cityofwinchestertrust.co.uk

www.winchester-cathedral.org.uk

www.visitwinchester.co.uk

www.research.hgt.org.uk

www.hants.gov.uk/greathall

www.childrenshomes.org.uk

www.hiddenlives.org.uk

www.hctcollections.org.uk (For Beatrice Olive Corfe watercolours)

Acknowledgements

We are most grateful to the following: the staff and volunteers of Winchester Cathedral for being so welcoming and so generous with their information; the staff at the Hampshire Record Office, in particular David Rymill for locating the piece on 'the Butterfly Bishop'; Dr Christina Welch from the University of Winchester and the Medieval Jewish Winchester Project for helpful advice and comments; Charlie, Stewart, Olivia, Katy and Ben for putting up with disruption to normal family life; in particular we would like to thank our friends Karen Quaddy and Clare Wallis for their invaluable help with proofing.

Images

All photographs and illustrations are the authors' own with the exception of the following:

Middle Brook Street, artist Samuel Prout, by kind permission of the Mayor of Winchester, City of Winchester;

Photo of Wolvesey Palace, Tony Hisgett, Wikimedia Commons;

Image of Stephen of England and Henry II, released by British Library Images Online;

Portrait of Mary I, Hans Eworth, Dickinson Gallery, Wikimedia Commons;

Photo of Queen Mary's chair reproduced from original Francis Frith & Co postcard;

Photo of the Round Table, Martin Kraft, Wikimedia Commons;

St Mary Magdalen Hospital, illustration from The History & Antiquities of Winchester, 1773;

Miniature by Pierart dou Tielt c. 1353, Diaspora Museum, Tel Aviv, Public Domain;

Illustration of Richard I, Matthew Paris, Wikimedia Commons;

Photo of Winnall Down Camp credited to Steve and Jenny Jarvis

Tanks on Winchester Bypass from the collections of the Imperial War Museum/ Wikimedia Commons;

Photo of the first Charabanc Outing from the Chisnell Family Collection by courtesy of the Friends of King Alfred Buses.

Authors' photographs of the Bishop Gardiner's Chantry Chapel, the Holy Sepulchre Chapel, and Peter des Roches tomb reproduced by kind permission of Winchester Cathedral.